Country of Nationality of those of whom's kin
inspired and encouraged the development of

CW00401218

America   Antigua   Argentina   Australia

China   Egypt   England   France   Germany   India

Ireland   Italy   Morocco   Nepal   Northern Ireland   Romania

Russia   Scotland   Spain   South Africa   Switzerland   United Kingdom

And to Jack for the inspiration of how clever a child can be at a very young age.

Special Thanks to
East Rhidorroch Estate and the Hastings Hotels Group

About the Author / Illustrator
Ann Quinn raced with the classical sailors in the Cannes Régates Royales,
Antigua Classics Regatta and crossed the Atlantic by classical sailboat in 2013,
a journey which inspired the creation of the "A Special Alphabet Adventure" book.

A British Council International Business graduate of Saint Leo University USA,
Computer Science graduate of Queens University, UK and European Media Business School graduate
of Multi-platform and Marketing and Distribution with placement to Paramount Studios, Sydney,
Ann worked as Northern Ireland Screen's Production Executive from 2004 - 2012 working with
national and international production companies on a range of productions from
HBO's GAME OF THRONES and Universal Studio's YOUR HIGHNESS to
Warp Film's Camera D'Or winning HUNGER and first films from indigenous filmmakers.

Ann wrote and oil painted the "A Special Alphabet Adventure" book between 2014 - 2016
whilst creating graphic paintings for the title sequence of ITV"s FRANKENSTEIN CHRONICLES and
completing freelance work for delivery to UTV, Electric Ireland and Disney. Her oil paintings have been
exhibited in New York and Ireland and are held in collections across Europe and the USA.

Caitlin Ryan managed the development of and art directed the "A Special Alphabet Adventure" book.
In the future, she hopes to travel and work in the creative sector.

First Edition Printing 2014. Text and Illustrations Copyright © Ann Quinn 2017. The moral right of the author has been asserted.
All rights reserved. Without limiting the rights under copyright reserved above, no part of this publication may be reproduced,
stored in or introduced into a retrieval system, or transmitted, in any form or by any means (electronic, mechanical,
photocopying, recording or otherwise), without the prior written permission of the copyright owner.

Inspire   Educate   Encourage   Special   Explore

A is for Ava

Special child, you are in here too
Because you will always be important
To those who love and care for you.

Reach high and follow all you love
And happy you will be;
Think in your head, "I CAN do it!"
You will be able to, you will see

My flag has the colours

Red Orange Yellow Green Blue Turquoise Navy

Violet Maroon Pink Beige Bronze Peach Purple

Brown Silver Gold White Grey Black

My favourite page is the

A Page B Page C Page D Page E Page F Page

G Page H Page I Page J Page K Page L Page M Page

N Page O Page P Page Q Page R Page S Page

T Page U Page V Page W Page X Page Y Page Z Page

B is for Bell
It made him terribly sad and grumpy,
That you could not talk to those
Living in a far off country.

UK Flag

Alexander Graham Bell
British (Scottish) Inventor

So he made a machine
That we now call the phone,
So where ever you are
You can always call home.

Famous for the invention of the
Telephone patented in 1876

Scottish Flag

C is for Cook

Sailing his boat on high seas new,
To find many super cool things
Across and under the sea of blue.

UK Flag

James Cook
British (English) Explorer and Sailor

English Flag

When his boat got stuck on a coral
Under the water he saw beneath,
Beautiful fishes and colours
Now called The Great Barrier Reef.

Famous for the first European landing at
Australia's Great Barrier Reef in 1770

Australian Flag

D is for Darwin
He would wonder all night and day;
Had people and animals
Always looked the same way?

UK Flag

Charles Darwin
British (English)
Naturalist

Famous for The Theory of Evolution
first published in 1859

Living things change shape
To find a clever solution,
Over millions of years,
And it is called Evolution.

Darwin's Finches: Guadeloupe Island was invaded by bigger birds
who stole all the little finches food. Over time, the finches beaks grew
smaller to eat the smaller nuts that the bigger birds could not eat.

English Flag

E is for Edison
Bored of the candle at night;
With wires and glass
Made a bulb of light.

American Flag

Thomas Edison
American Inventor

He made the first camera
Now we have photographs too
Bringing back good memories
If ever you feel blue.

Famous for the invention of the Light Bulb patented in 1879
and for the invention of the Camera patented in 1891

F is for Fleming

He made a magic pill,
That people would take
To stop feeling ill.

UK Flag

Sir Alexander Fleming
British (Scottish) Pharmacologist

Scottish Flag

**Famous for the
invention of
Penicillin in 1928**

On a dish by a window
Some greeny blue mould grew,
With microscope and potions
His super pill dream came true.

German Flag

Penicillin (the world's 1st antibiotic) was purified in
development by Sir Howard Florey (Australian) and
Sir Ernst Boris Chain (British / German-born / Refugee)

Australian Flag

G is for Gandhi

He told his people not to fight;
NO, dear Indian people,
It really is not right.

Indian Flag

Mahatma Gandhi
Indian Peacemaker

You do not need to shout and fuss
Tell the truth and you can,
You are so very much stronger,
On the inside when you are calm.

Famous as a Leader promoting peaceful ways
commonly known as Satyagraha (meaning loyalty to the truth)
to a large group of Indian people in 1906

H is for Hillary

He loved climbing mountains big and small
And one day he dreamed,
He would climb the biggest of them all.

New Zealand Flag

Sir Edmund Hillary
New Zealand Mountaineer

Guided by Nepalese Sherpa
Tenzing Norgay

Nepalese Flag

His Sherpa helped to show the way
And with his axe and his super warm vest,
He was first to climb to the very top
Of The Great Mount Everest.

Famous for being the first climbers to reach Mount Everest's Summit in 1953

I is for Isaac Newton

An apple fell down on his head.
It made him think; why had it not
Flown up to the sky instead?

UK Flag

Sir Isaac Newton
British (English) Physicist and Mathematician

The apple pulls the earth a little
The earth pulls the apple more you see,
So the much bigger earth, wins the tug of war,
From the pull of the earth's gravity.

Famous for writing Principia Mathematica
(The Three Laws of Motion) first published in 1687

English Flag

J is for **Joan** of Arc
She followed a dream she had one night;
An angel told her she must go now
To help King Charles to fight.

French Flag

Joan of Arc
A Young French Heroine

A cunning plan, dressed up as a boy
Cutting her hair so she would get in;
For Joan was to lead the battle
That, in just nine days, they would win.

Famous for leading the French against the English in the
"100 years war" and winning the
"Siege of Orléans" in just 9 days in 1429

K is for Keller

She could not see or hear at all;
It made her so upset
She smashed her favourite doll.

American Flag

Helen Keller
American Author

One day she thought, "I cannot see..
But I feel this water on my hand."
So touching shapes raised on a board
She found a way to understand.

Famous for breaking through the isolation of deaf and blindness
to become the first deaf and blind person to earn a degree in 1904

L is for Langley
By the river far and wide
Thought boats can not be the only way
To reach the other side.

American Flag

Samuel Pierpont Langley
American
Aviation Pioneer

A catapult on the hill
Put his plane into the sky,
Bell clapped and took the photo
As soon people would fly.

Famous for the first flight of an un piloted engine driven aircraft "Aerodrome No. 5" launched from a catapult over the Potomac River in 1896. The flight was photographed by Alexander Graham Bell and followed Newton's Laws of motion .

M is for Mozart
He loved music so very much
He would play the piano
With the lightest of touch.

Austrian Flag

Wolfgang Amadeus Mozart
Austrian Composer and Musician

He would spend all his time
Writing music all day,
That forever in many lands
Musicians would play.

Famous for his classical music compositions such as "A Little Serenade" and
"Piano Concerto No 20" created between 1756 and 1791

N is for Nightingale

They called her, "The Lady of the Lamp."
A nurse working hard to help
The sick of the war camp.

UK Flag

Florence Nightingale
British (English) Nurse

She made the world a better place
Wrong doings she would put right;
And to make sure everyone was well,
She would work right through the night.

Famous as the Founder of Nursing between 1820 and 1910

English Flag

O is for Owens

He would run fast and jump far;
At the world's biggest race
He became quite the star.

American Flag

Jesse Owens
American Athlete

Some said words to hurt him
But Owen's was not fazed,
A winning streak of four times gold,
The crowd watched on amazed.

Famous for one of the greatest performances in Olympic history
setting three world records and tying another in under an hour
amidst negative racial commentary at the 1936 games

P is for Pankhurst

She lived in a day
Where only a boy,
Could have any say.

UK Flag

Emmeline Pankhurst
British (English) Suffragette

English Flag

It made her so sad
Her life she would devote;
So both boys and girls
Would have the right to vote.

Famous for her work towards achieving voting rights
for women between 1858 and 1928

Q is for **Queen** Elizabeth the First
A United Kingdom Queen.
She would send sailors across the sea
To places they had never been.

UK Flag

Queen Elizabeth the First
Famous Royal

And when the sailors came back home
They had new things for you and me;
Bright cloth, spices and sugar
Some chocolate and coffee.

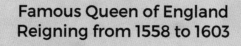

Famous Queen of England
Reigning from 1558 to 1603

English Flag

R is for **Roald** Amundsen
Loving polar bears and snow;
Went off to explore the Antarctic
And reached the North and South Pole.

Norwegian Flag

Roald Amundsen
Norwegian Explorer

Robert Falcon Scott
British Explorer

UK Flag

At the South a man was close behind
But Roald was first to get there;
Finding penguins near the South Pole
The North home of The Great Polar Bear.

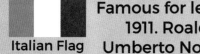

Italian Flag

Famous for leading the expedition to see the first men at the South Pole in 1911. Roald also reached the North Pole in 1926 with Italian Explorer Umberto Nobile making him the first man to reach the ends of the earth.

S is for Shakespeare

He would write stories on a page,
Which actors would then
Play out on a stage.

UK Flag

William Shakespeare
British (English) Playwright and Actor

English Flag

Crowds would come and watch for fun;
There were no televisions then you see.
They would laugh and hear the famous line;
"To be or not to be."

Famous for writing the plays Hamlet, Macbeth and
Romeo and Juliet created between 1564 and 1616

T is for **Tim** Berners-Lee

It was not a very long time ago;
You only had a library book
To find what you needed to know.

UK Flag

Sir Tim Berners-Lee
British (English) Inventor

English Flag

There was no social media
You read a book, wrote a letter, that was that;
So Tim invented the World Wide Web
Making it easier to learn and chat.

Famous for the invention of the World Wide Web in 1989

U is for Ulyssés

Myth or truth, which will it be?
A Greek hero in an epic book
By Homer called Odyssey.

Greek Flag

**Ulyssés
Greek Hero**

Famous in Greek Mythology as The King of Ithaca
who took over a decade to return home
after the 10 year long Trojan War

As legend goes, he built a giant horse
And with his men he crept inside;
So the castle let down it's drawbridge
Thinking it was just a horse outside!

Homer
Greek Poet
and Author

Famous as the author of
potentially the first known
literature in Europe in 850

Greek Flag

V is for Van Gogh

Painting in colours of oil so bright;
From sunflowers to bedrooms
To bright stars in the sky at night.

Dutch Flag

Vincent Van Gogh
Dutch Painter

One day all over the world
His paintings were to be
Hanging in museums
For everyone to see.

Famous for his special oil painting style and art
created between 1853 and 1890

W is for Winston Churchill

At leading he was best.
The days were very sad back then
Which put him to the test.

UK Flag

Winston Churchill
Prime Minister of the United Kingdom

He gave the people words to think of
When the days were very long;
So instead of feeling low inside
They were happy as they felt strong.

Famous for his leadership throughout
World War 2 between 1939 and 1945

English Flag

X is the spot
Martin Luther-King made his mark
Saying people should work together
Should their skin be light or dark.

American Flag

Martin Luther-King Jr
American Civil Rights Activist

"I have a dream" Martin said aloud
Soon equality would start;
Your skin colour's not important,
It's the good that's in your heart.

Famous for the iconic "I Have a Dream" speech
promoting race equality in 1963

Y is for Yeats
His words music to the ear,
That people loved to listen to
They would come from far and near.

Irish Flag

W. B. Yeats
Irish Poet

He would tell of moths flying in the sky
Like they were sparks of light;
Of fallen berries and river banks
And glittering fish by night.

Famous for his inspiring poetry and awarded
The Nobel Prize for Literature in 1923

Z is for ZZZZzz
Time to go to sleep now
And dream of all things,
Wonder who, when or how?

The adventures you will go on
Fun you will have and things you will see
And remember you are always special
Because you are special to me.

22121560R00032

Printed in Great Britain
by Amazon